Brat Packs

Flower Power!

Written by
Gaby Goldsack

Hippo

Scholastic Children's Books,
Commonwealth House, 1-19 New Oxford Street,
London WC1A 1NU, UK
a division of Scholastic Ltd
London ~ New York ~ Toronto ~ Sydney ~ Auckland

First published by Scholastic Ltd, 1997

ISBN 0 590 19099 7

Printed by Cox & Wyman Ltd, Reading, Berks.

Contents:

Flower Power

Congratulations! You are now the proud owner
of a fantastic Flower Power pack. With the help
of this book and the seeds that come with it (you
know, those strange knobbly things stuck to the
front of this book) you can really get down to
earth and get growing.

Take a close look and you'll find tomato, nasturtium and sunflower seeds, just waiting for you to give them a bit of life. Now all you need is a pot, some soil and a little TLC (tender loving care – you know, that stuff that your parents smother you with) and you'll be up to your eyeballs in flowers and green, leafy things. In fact, it could be said that this book gives you the ultimate in Flower Power!

You will notice that there are quite a few seeds. Don't worry, you're not expected to grow bumper crops. In fact, it is very unlikely that all of your seeds will grow. Some seeds just don't have any Flower Power in them, so don't give up if you have a few failures.

This book isn't just about growing things. The great thing about these seeds is that you can actually pig out on the end results. Even bits of the nasturtium can be transformed into tasty snacks. AND there are lots of other things for you to make, do and read about while you wait for your plants to perform.

Don't worry if you haven't got a garden. Even if you only have a small patch of concrete where the dustbin is normally dumped, or half shares in the tiniest of windowsills you could soon be the owner of a flowery haven. Even if you live in a cardboard box in the middle of the Antarctic you are in with a fighting chance that SOMETHING will grow! So, read on, start sowing and get ready for some fantastic results!

A few words about FLOWER POWER

Just so that you know – Flower Power cannot be used to power your Sega, television, video or even your mum's car. However, it can be used to bring a little happiness into people's dull and boring lives. Ahhh. Isn't that nice? If you're not convinced by all this lovey dovey nonsense, or it leaves you feeling sick, don't worry. The most important thing is that Flower Power is really good fun.

None of the things in this book are very difficult to do, but some are a bit more tricky than others. Some are so incredibly easy and quick that it's almost cheating. So to let you know exactly what you're letting yourself in for, look for one of these signs next to each activity:

cheat   easy   not so easy   adult

What you will need

It's a good idea to start by gathering some of the things that you'll need for the activities in this book. Hopefully you'll be able to get your hands on them without spending too much dosh!

Newspaper Spread this all over the place before you start doing any messy work but do make sure your dad's finished reading it first!

Flowerpots Keen gardeners normally have loads of these stashed away, so start asking around. If you can't get your mitts on any, try using other sorts of containers – even a smelly old trainer will do!

Compost This is a special sort of gardening soil mixed with all sorts of goodies to help plants grow. Gardeners, or even just houseplant lovers, normally have some lurking around, but if not it should be fairly cheap to buy from your local garden centre. If you've already spent your pocket money, it's always worth trying just ordinary old soil – with luck something should grow!

Watering can All plants need watering but you don't need a fancy container to do this – any container will do!

Polythene bags Transparent polythene bags tied over flowerpots make a nice little home for your seeds to start germinating (sprouting) in. The sort that supermarket veggies come in should be fine!

Sticks Tomatoes and sunflowers will need sticks to support their stems as they grow taller. Look around for bamboo canes or any other sturdy sticks.

Elastic bands or string These are useful for securing polythene bags over your pots and for tying stems to sticks.

Pips Start collecting any pips and seeds that you think you may be able to grow into something. This book will give you a few ideas but the secret is, if you think it might grow, have a go and see!

Glue stick Towards the end of the book you will find lots of fantastic things to make. For some of them you will need glue and we think you'll find that a glue stick is pretty clean and effective.

Paints There's got to be at least one excuse to crack open the paint pot. See if you can get hold of some ceramic paint to create your very own Flower Power pot (see page 56).

Scissors and craft knives Take care when you are using these as your parents probably won't want you bleeding all over the carpet.

Scraps of coloured paper Always worth collecting even if you're not sure exactly what you're going to do with them.

A grown-up Where you see the grown-up sign, you will probably need to use one. They are usually pretty easy to find – just head for the person with the bossiest voice and the chances are you'll have found a grown-up.

Pots of Fun

Sunflowers

Sunflowers have it all – good looks, personality and lots and lots of growing power! They can grow from tiny seedlings to enormous monsters – sometimes as tall as a two-storey house – in just six short months. Not only that – they're really easy to grow, too. What more could a budding botanist (that's you) ask for?

Sunflower power

The best time to sow your sunflower seeds indoors is early spring. You'll know when it's spring because your mum will start insisting that you clear out all those rotting apple cores from underneath your bed and demand that you give your room a SPRING clean!

<u>You will need</u>

- ✿ **old newspaper to cover work surface**
- ✿ **some large flowerpots**
- ✿ **compost**
- ✿ **a watering can or jug**
- ✿ **sunflower seeds**
- ✿ **polythene bags**
- ✿ **string or elastic bands**
- ✿ **sticks**

1. Cover your work surface with the newspaper to avoid making too much of a mess, then fill the flowerpots with compost and water well.

2. Use your finger to make a hole about 2 cm deep in the centre of each pot, then pop a seed into each hole. It's normally a good idea to wash your hands after poking around in compost as composty fingers take all the fun out of picking your nose and a sprinkle of compost doesn't really do much for your lunchtime sandwiches.

3. Cover the seeds with more compost, then water again. But be careful not to drown the seeds or you'll be waiting a long time to see anything sprout.

4. Cover each pot with a see-through polythene bag and tie it on with string or elastic bands.

5. Place on a sunny windowsill and wait.

You don't have to keep watch 24 hours a day!

6. After about two weeks the first shoots should begin to appear. Remove the polythene bag and very carefully push a stick into the soil next to each plant, and loosely tie the plant to it with cotton or string.

7. Water your plants whenever the soil becomes dry and watch them grow. You will need to tie them with extra string from time to time. Very soon you could have a monster on your hands.

Sunflowers are real sun worshippers. Once they begin to flower, take a look at them at different times of the day. No, you aren't going mad, they really do move around so that they're always facing the sun!

❀ ❀ ❀ Tip ❀ ❀ ❀
It's best not to water any plant when the sun is hot. Wait until early evening.

Sunflower garden

If you are lucky enough to have a garden of your own, you will find growing sunflowers an outrageously easy job. The best time to sow them outside is in the spring, but they can be sown as late as July.

You will need

✿ **a sunny, sheltered plot of land**

✿ **seeds**

✿ **a watering can or jug**

✿ **a stick**

✿ **string**

1. Find a nice sunny spot that is sheltered from the wind (make sure that it's not the same place that your dad's decided to sow his prize pumpkins). Poke holes in the soil about 2cm deep and 60cm apart. Pop the seeds straight in, then cover them with soil and water gently – whatever you do, don't drown the seeds in a tidal wave of water.

2. When the first shoots begin to appear, very gently push a large cane beside each plant and tie loosely with string. You must be very careful when you do this or your plant will get damaged and your chances of growing a prize sunflower will be dashed.

3. Water regularly and add extra string ties from time to time. Loosen old ties as the stem becomes thicker.

4. With any luck your sunflowers should flower between July and September. Who knows, you could even have a record breaker on your hands!

Sunflower race

Growing monster sunflowers can be record-breaking fun. Why not have a race with a friend to see who can grow the tallest, and who can grow the one with the largest flower? The height should be measured from ground level to the very highest petal. The flower should be measured from the tip of a petal one side to the tip of a petal the other side. Decide on a date late in the summer for them to be measured and start growing.

Did you know?
The tallest recorded sunflower was grown in the Netherlands in 1986 – it grew to an amazing 7 metres. And a sunflower with a head measuring a breath-taking 82cm was grown in Canada in 1983.

Sunflowers are really useful plants – not only are their seeds used for many different things, but other parts of it are pretty useful too. The stalks can be made into paper and the pith inside the stalks is one of the lightest substances known – it has even been used in lifebelts. Even the petals don't go to waste – they are used to make some paints yellow!

Nasturtium know-how

Nasturtiums are another fun flower to grow, though don't expect them to reach for the skies like sunflowers! BUT, they are ridiculously easy to grow – they're not fussy about the sort of soil they grow in, and they shoot up in no time at all. Like the sunflower, you can plant them straight into the soil in late spring if you have a garden, but why not go crazy and experiment a little? You can sow them in window boxes, in hanging baskets, in plain old pots – or you could go blooming mad and plant them in something wacky like an old boot, a hat, a teapot, a potty, a cuddly toy ... (well, perhaps not a cuddly toy, but lots of other things)!

Balls of fun

Next time your dog (or even your kid brother) sinks his fangs into your favourite football, don't throw it away – use it to make an attractive hat or (even better) sow some nasturtium seeds in it.

You will need

❀ a punctured football (or anything else you think would make a good container)

❀ a sharp knife to make holes

❀ newspaper

❀ soil (any old stuff should do)

❀ your nasturtium seeds

❀ watering can or jug

❀ a sunny windowsill

1. Get your grown-up to cut one large hole in your football to make the mouth of your pot, and some smaller ones for drainage on the opposite side.

17

2. Cover your surface with newspaper and fill the ball with soil, then water it. Make holes in the soil about 1cm deep, 5cm apart and pop a single seed in each one. Cover with soil, then water.

3. Place on a sunny windowsill, water regularly and wait for the plants to appear. If the baby plants look a little on the cramped side, carefully pick a few out and put them into another container. With luck you should have orange or yellow flowers from June onwards! Blooming lovely!

Nasturtiums are pretty weird-looking flowers. They are kind of trumpet shaped with five petals and a strange spur sticking out the back!

Basket case

If you have any nasturtium seeds left over why not grow them in this hanging basket, made out of a large plastic bottle?

<u>You will need</u>

✿ **a large plastic bottle with screwcap**

✿ **scissors**

✿ **fine sandpaper**

✿ **strong string**

✿ **newspaper**

✿ **small stones**

✿ **your nasturtium seeds**

✿ **soil**

✿ **a strong hook**

✿ **a watering can or jug**

1. Get your grown-up to cut the bottom half of the bottle off with the scissors. Remove the screwcap and turn the top half of the bottle upside down and you'll see that you have the makings of a tiny hanging basket. Use the sandpaper to smooth down any rough edges there might be.

2. Cut three long lengths of string to make a holder for the basket to hang in. Fold two of these lengths in half to find the middle, then tie a loop in them large enough for the bottle's neck to slip through.

3. Push these two loops over the neck of the bottle so they cradle the basket, as shown.

4. Now tie the third piece of string actually around the basket, knotting it to each of the four string supports to secure.

5. Tie a loop where the four string ends meet at the top and, hey presto, you have a totally terrific hanging basket just waiting to give a home to your seeds.

20

6. Now cover your work surface with newspaper (though make sure everyone's read it first!). Then block the hole in the neck of the bottle with a few small stones, chuck in some soil and plant your seeds.

7. Hang outside from a sturdy nail or hook and water regularly. Before you know it, you should have a colourful hanging garden outside your own front door!

Like sunflowers and tomatoes, nasturtiums are what gardeners call annuals. No, this doesn't mean that they are one of those bumper comic books that always turn up in your Christmas stocking. In the world of plants being an annual means that a plant grows, flowers and dies in one season. So unless you harvest some seeds you can't expect your nasturtium, sunflower or tomatoes to grow year after year! Find out how to do this on pages 34, 38 and 39.

Tasty tomatoes

Sow your tomato seeds in early spring and you could be feasting on them all summer long!

<u>You will need</u>

* ✿ newspaper
* ✿ flowerpots
* ✿ compost
* ✿ tomato seeds
* ✿ a water sprayer
  (also fun for squirting your mates)
* ✿ polythene bags
* ✿ string or elastic bands
* ✿ a large pot
* ✿ a watering can
* ✿ sticks
* ✿ special tomato feed
  (useful but not totally vital)

1. Cover your work surface with newspaper, fill the small pots with compost and then water. Pop a couple of seeds in each pot and cover with about 20mm of compost. Spray with water so that the compost is damp but not soggy.

2. Cover each pot with a polythene bag and secure with string or an elastic band. Place pots on a sunny windowsill. Spray the compost from time to time to keep it damp.

3. After about two weeks they should begin to sprout. Remove the polythene bag and leave on the windowsill until the plants are about 5cm tall. Pick out any weedy-looking plants so that each pot contains just one plant. This will let the plants really get growing!

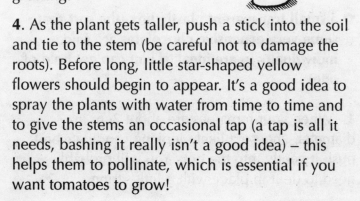

4. As the plant gets taller, push a stick into the soil and tie to the stem (be careful not to damage the roots). Before long, little star-shaped yellow flowers should begin to appear. It's a good idea to spray the plants with water from time to time and to give the stems an occasional tap (a tap is all it needs, bashing it really isn't a good idea) – this helps them to pollinate, which is essential if you want tomatoes to grow!

5. After a short time, you should notice tiny tomatoes growing at the base of the dying flowers. When they do, you can start feeding them with tomato feed if you have any. You will know when the tomatoes are ready to pick because they will turn a lovely red colour!

Square deal

It might seem unbelievable, but you can actually grow square tomatoes. Just think, no more rattling about in your lunch box.

<u>You will need</u>

✿ **a tomato plant**

✿ **a small transparent plastic box (the sort that some very expensive chocolates are sold individually in are ideal, if you can get hold of one)**

1. When your tomatoes are about 2cm in diameter, choose a likely-looking candidate and push it gently into the box. You will probably need to tie it in place with a little string.

24

2. Wait for the tomato to grow and ripen. When the tomato has almost filled the plastic box, remove the string.

3. Pick the boxed tomato, then gently slide it out of the box. Wow, a square tomato (well nearly)!

Tomatoes originally come from South America. When they made their way into Britain in the late 1500s, they were treated with suspicion. People thought that they were poisonous and it was almost 200 years before they made it to the dinner table!

Eat Your Work

One of the best things about growing the succulent seeds that come with this book is that you can actually eat all your hard work! Now is the time to get cooking!

Scrummy sunflowers

<u>You will need</u>

✿ **a stepladder or chair**

✿ **a wood saw**

✿ **a tray**

✿ **a baking tray**

✿ **a hot oven**

1. When the petals of your sunflowers begin to shrivel and the seed shells feel hard, get your grown-up to clamber up on a stepladder or chair and saw the flowerhead off.

2. If the weather is fine, leave the heads to dry in the sun for about a week. Then use your hands, or a fork, to rub all the seeds onto a tray. Spread them out and leave on a sunny windowsill for another week until they're completely dry. If it's not that sunny, you might have to leave them out for longer.

3. Now take some of the juiciest-looking seeds, put them on a baking tray and cook in the oven for 10 minutes at 200°C/400°F/Gas Mark 6.

4. Once they're roasted, leave them to cool then remove their shells. Now dig in to a delicious snack.

Once you have roasted your sunflower seeds and removed their shells, they can be used for many other things besides snacking material. Try sprinkling them over a salad to give it a delicious nutty flavour. Sprinkled on top of cakes or biscuits they give a really satisfying munch.

Wimpier-looking seeds can be left out on the bird table or hung from a tree to feed the birds when winter comes.

Don't forget to save a few of your sunflower seeds so that you can sow some again next year. After you've dried them, simply slip them into an airtight container (an old film canister is pretty good) and keep them in a cool place. Just think, you can have sunflowers year after year without ever having to buy another seed!

Nifty nasturtiums

To the average gardener, nasturtiums are simply a stunning summer flower. But to you they could soon become a scrummy supper! The young leaves have a slightly peppery flavour and the flowers can add a spot of colour to any salad!

Salad surprise

serves 2–4

You will need

- ✿ **200 g cooked rice**
- ✿ **½ chopped cucumber**
- ✿ **a handful of sunflower shoots (optional)**
- ✿ **2 chopped tomatoes (optional)**
- ✿ **a few tender young nasturtium leaves**
- ✿ **a salad bowl**
- ✿ **1 tablespoon mayonnaise**
- ✿ **sunflower seeds (optional)**
- ✿ **a few nasturtium flowers**

1. Wash all the fresh ingredients in cold water and chuck the rice, cucumber, sunflower shoots, tomatoes and nasturtium leaves into the salad bowl.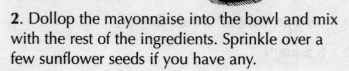

2. Dollop the mayonnaise into the bowl and mix with the rest of the ingredients. Sprinkle over a few sunflower seeds if you have any.

3. Now add the surprise – that little something extra that is going to make this a salad to remember – that's right, the nasturtium flowers. Whoever said salads were boring?

Nasturtium flowers also look great in fruit salad!

Stuffed flowers

For the more adventurous scoffer, stuffed nasturtium flowers make a really unusual snack!

makes 4

<u>You will need</u>

✿ **2 tender young nasturtium leaves**

✿ **a knife**

✿ **a large tablespoon of cream cheese**

✿ **a mixing bowl**

✿ **a fork**

✿ **4 well-grown nasturtium flowers**

✿ **a teaspoon**

1. Chop the nasturtium leaves finely, then pop them into the mixing bowl with the cream cheese. Mix thoroughly with the fork – go on, put some welly into it!

2. Now very carefully spoon a small teaspoonful of the mixture into each flower head, taking care not to break any petals!

3. Served up with a few nasturtium leaves for decoration, this makes a lunchtime snack with a difference!

Flowery ice-cubes

To put the final touch to a cool summery drink, make ice-cubes with some of the smaller nasturtium flowers.

You will need

✿ **small nasturtium flowers**

✿ **an ice-cube tray**

✿ water

✿ a freezer

1. Simply pop washed flowers into the ice-cube tray and fill with water.

2. Freeze and serve up in any cool summer drink!

What a caper!

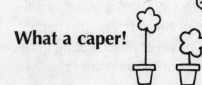

Do you like capers? You know, those strange salty things which sometimes turn up on pizzas or in sauces. Even if you don't, perhaps you know someone who does. If you do, you could try pickling a few nasturtium seeds as they taste a lot like capers.

<u>You will need</u>

✿ **a nasturtium plant**

✿ **a sterilized jar**

✿ **pickling vinegar**

1. When the petals fall from your nasturtium flowers, harvest a few of the green seeds and give them a good wash.

2. Sterilize your jar by filling it with boiling water and leaving to cool (make sure your grown-up is around for this bit). Boil some vinegar, keeping a careful eye on it at all times.

3. Pour the cooled water out of the jar, and pack it with the green seeds, then get a grown-up to pour the boiling vinegar over them, filling the jar.

4. Seal the jar and store in a cool place. The seeds should be ready within a few days, so go on – give them a go! You might not like them, but they would make an unusual pressie – someone out there must like them!

By the way, unless you want to win a vomiting competition or have a strange desire to spend the night on the toilet, it's not a good idea to eat just any old seed. Some of them are POISONOUS and visiting your local hospital is never pleasant!

Don't scoff all your nasturtium flowers and seeds, leave some of the seeds on the plant until they turn brown and dry. Then pick them off and store them in a cool, dark place ready for starting all over again next year.

Tremendous tomatoes

There's only one part of the tomato that we're interested in eating and that's the lovely plump fruit. Don't even think about trying the leaves or you could be rushing to the nearest doctor! But, there are loads of things that you can make with tasty toms.

Perfect pizza

serves 2–4

<u>You will need</u>

To make the tomato sauce

✿ **1 small onion, chopped**

✿ **2 tablespoons vegetable oil**

✿ **4 ripe tomatoes, chopped finely**

✿ **salt and pepper**

For the base

✿ **small French stick, cut in half lengthways**

For topping

❀ **113g of grated mozzarella or Cheddar cheese**

1. Very carefully heat the oil in a saucepan, then add the onion and fry for about 10 minutes.

2. Add the chopped tomatoes and cook for another 10 minutes. Season with salt and pepper to taste.

3. Spread this tomato sauce evenly over the French bread, then sprinkle with the cheese.

4. Pop under a low grill for about 10 minutes. Now it's pizza all round!

Pour the same sauce over cooked pasta for a quick and tasty meal!

Get stuffed!

If you manage to grow any largish tomatoes, why not stuff them for a special treat?

serves 2

<u>You will need</u>

✿ **an oven**

✿ **4 large tomatoes**

✿ **57g of breadcrumbs**

✿ **113g of grated cheese**

✿ **a mixing bowl**

✿ **salt and pepper**

✿ **½ tablespoon oil**

✿ **a greased baking tray**

1. Get a grown-up to set an oven at 190°C/ 375°F/Gas Mark 5. Carefully cut the tomatoes in half and dig out the goo. Turn the tomato halves upside down and put to one side while you get on with the rest of the stuff.

2. Chop up the gooey part of the tomato and mix with the fresh breadcrumbs and grated cheese. Season with a good shake of the salt and pepper.

3. Stuff the tomato halves with the filling then put them on the baking tray. Dribble a little oil on each one (olive oil is really nice) and pop into the oven.

4. Bake for about 25 minutes, then remove the tomatoes from the oven. Leave them to cool for a while, then serve up (if you can wait that long).

Delicious!

Tomatoes need lots of sun to ripen. If by the end of the summer, there are a few greenies left lurking around, bring them indoors and try to ripen them on a windowsill. If they still don't ripen, persuade your folks to make them into chutney.

Seeds for free

If you want to harvest a few tomato seeds to sow again next year, you could be in for a lot of gooey fun!

You will need

✿ **a few overripe tomatoes, on plant**

✿ **a jar**

✿ **a spoon**

✿ **water**

✿ **a sieve**

1. Leave some ripe tomatoes on the plant until they're good and squishy – we're talking 'squashed tomatoes in your face' time here (well, you can use a few of them to chuck at unsuspecting mates if you want, but don't use them all). Pick the overripe tomatoes.

2. Cut them open and scoop the seeds and the jelly-like liquid into a jar. Leave this gooey mess in a warm spot for a few days and allow a lovely furry mat of mould to grow.

3. After four days scoop off the furry mould with a spoon. Add water to the jar and pour the whole lot through a sieve.

4. Wash the seeds under a running tap until they're squeaky clean. They'll probably look rather hairy at this stage but don't panic – this is the way they're meant to look.

5. Spread them on a plate and leave them to dry somewhere out of the sun. Then pop them into an envelope and hang them somewhere to dry out completely for two weeks. Store them in a cool dark place until next year. Don't forget to label them!

Tomato seeds

Potty about Plants

By now you are probably feeling Flower Power crazy and just itching to get your hands on some more seeds. But before you go dashing to your local garden centre, have a quick rummage through your rubbish.

Yes, that's right, you can actually grow loads of exotic houseplants from things that you would usually throw away. Just think of all those apple, orange, melon and lime pips that go to waste! Then there's things like avocado and date stones. AND you can even grow plants from scraps such as carrot and pineapple tops. All that stands between you and a house full of freebie foliage are a few pips or kitchen discards and a little bit of patience.

Orange tree

Most people munch their way through quite a few oranges so you're sure to be able to get your hands on some of their pips pretty easily. They're quite easy to grow and make brilliant plants.

<u>You will need</u>

✿ **newspaper**

✿ **fresh orange pips**

✿ **pots**

✿ **compost**

✿ **a watering can or jug**

✿ **a polythene bag**

✿ **an elastic band or string**

1. Cover your work surfaces with newspaper and fill the pots with compost. Use your finger to poke a hole about 1cm deep in each pot. Pop a pip into each hole and cover with compost.

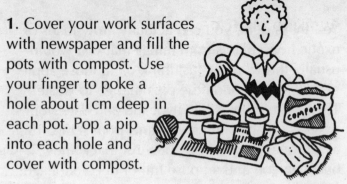

2. Water with slightly warm water, then cover the pots with a see-through polythene bag. Use an elastic band or some string to secure in position.

3. Put the pot on a sunny windowsill and wait. Make sure that the compost doesn't dry out and within a month the first shoots should begin to come through. Unfortunately, some seeds will never sprout and no amount of TLC will coax them into life, so it's a good idea to plant loads of pips from a few different oranges. Once they do begin to sprout, remove the polythene bags, sit back and watch them grow! One day, you'll find yourself looking at a dinky little orange tree with cute little flowers and perhaps the odd fruit!

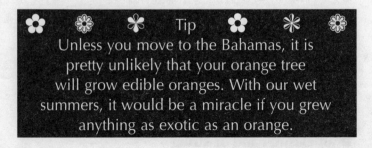

Tip

Unless you move to the Bahamas, it is pretty unlikely that your orange tree will grow edible oranges. With our wet summers, it would be a miracle if you grew anything as exotic as an orange.

Avocado plant

Growing avocado stones in water gives you a chance to actually watch a seed sprouting. As they like to be warm and snug, it is a good idea to grow them in winter when the radiators are on.

You will need

❀ **a stone from a nice ripe avocado**

❀ **a bowl of tepid water**

❀ **hairpins**

❀ **a jar of water**

❀ **a nice warm place**

❀ **a flowerpot**

❀ **soil-less potting compost**

❀ **a watering can or jug**

1. Leave the stone to soak in tepid water for 48 hours. Try to keep the water tepid by standing the bowl on a warm radiator or near a heater. This will make the avocado think it's in a warm climate!

2. Push two hairpins into the side of the stone, about halfway up. You might need to ask a

grown-up to pierce the
stone first with a skewer –
avocado stones can be
pretty tough when they
want to be!

3. Fill a jar with water and rest the avocado stone
over the mouth of the jar, with it's broad base
actually resting in the water. The hairpins should
act as supports.

4. Keep the jar topped up
with warm water so that
the base is always covered
and after a while a root
should begin to grow.
This can take anything
from 10 days to five weeks.

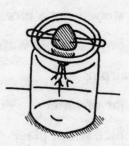

5. When there is a mass of roots, the plant is
ready to go into a pot. Pick it up by the stone and
hold it over the pot (you can remove the hairpins
now), with its tip just level with the pot's
rim. Carefully pour some compost
down among the roots,
then firm some around
the stone. Leave the top
half of the stone above
the compost. Now, sit
back and watch it grow.

Plants behaving badly

If you're feeling rich there are some gloriously gruesome plants that you can buy from garden centres. Look out for the Venus fly-trap (this one is definitely not for the faint-hearted) which actually feasts on flies. Its leaves are like hinged jaws that snap together when a fly brushes against a trigger.

The fly then becomes trapped inside by bar-like spikes which fringe the leaf. Now the plant gets down to its evil task of devouring its prey. Gooey juices leak out of the leaf and slowly dissolve the fly bit by bit until all that is left is a dried-up skin! Obviously, this is one to be ignored by fly lovers!

Another meat-loving plant is the pitcher plant. This bizarre-looking plant has dangling leaves that are rolled up to look and work rather like pitchers (or jugs). These pitchers contain a nasty, insect-dissolving liquid. To capture its prey, the plant sets a deadly trap of sweet nectar around the rim of the pitchers and just waits for some poor unsuspecting insect to come nibbling. When the insect has finished snacking and peers into the pitcher, it finds itself sliding on the smooth, slippery surface into the evil-looking juices below. Once inside, any escape is made impossible by sharp, pointed hairs. Before long the poor insect is drowned and the ghastly dissolving juices get to work. You will be relieved to know that there is no meat-eating plant large enough to make a meal of your average human being!

It's a date

Date stones feel as hard as stone and to tell you the truth, getting one to sprout can sometimes seem like trying to squeeze life out of a stone. But, if you are successful you can end up with a plant really worth boasting about.

<u>You will need</u>

✿ **loads of date stones
   (the sort that come from boxed dates are fine)**

✿ **water**

✿ compost

✿ a polythene bag

✿ an airing cupboard or other warm spot

✿ a small flowerpot

✿ a watering can or jug

1. When you've finished devouring your box of dates (you'll normally find a few of these lurking around at Christmas) soak the stones in tepid water for a couple of days.

2. Put a handful of damp compost into a polythene bag, lay the stones on this, then cover with another layer of damp compost.

3. Tie the top of the bag and put into the airing cupboard or other warm spot.

4. Sprinkle with water from time to time and keep an eye out for any roots. If any roots do appear, fill a small pot with compost and very carefully plant the stone, root facing down, about 1.5cm beneath the surface. Put on a sunny windowsill and water regularly. If the stones don't sprout within two months give them up as a lost cause and take up mud wrestling instead! If they do grow, now is the time to start boring your friends with your green-fingered know-how!

Do you have any idea how hard it is to grow a date plant?

yawn!

Hanging carrot top

Carrots might taste pretty yukky but they do have fantastic leafy foliage that looks great as a houseplant. For this hanging carrot you will need a HUGE healthy-looking specimen. And before you start rummaging through the freezer, THERE IS ABSOLUTELY NO WAY THAT YOU'RE GOING TO SQUEEZE ANY LIFE OUT OF ANYTHING FROZEN!

<u>You will need</u>

✿ **a large carrot, with top still intact**

✿ **a sharp knife**

✿ **a skewer**

✿ **string**

✿ **a watering can or jug**

You'll probably need your grown-up to help you with a lot of this.

1. Slice off the top 7-8cm of your carrot (so if your carrot is any smaller than this you're already in trouble).

2. Carefully remove the core (the inner circle of flesh) from the top, until it is hollow.

3. Use a skewer to carefully make three holes in the sides of the carrot top. Thread these holes with string so that the top hangs down – sort of like a miniature bucket. Find a place to hang the thing where people won't be continually knocking their heads against it (there really is nothing worse than a carrot in your eye).

4. Fill the hollow part of the carrot with water. Keep it topped up with fresh water and if you're lucky carrotty ferns will begin to sprout from the bottom. If you're not so lucky, the whole thing will go rotten and the place will begin to pong. If this happens, use your failure to taunt your kid brother and start again with a new carrot.

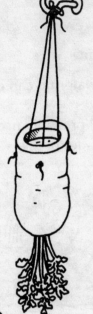

Potted pineapple

Fresh pineapples (we're definitely not talking about the tinned variety here) are not only delicious to eat, the top part can also be used to make a plant that will amaze your friends and family.

<u>You will need</u>

✿ **fresh pineapple, with spiky leaves in place**

✿ **a sharp knife**

✿ **newspaper**

✿ **compost**

✿ **a handful of sand**

✿ **a large pot**

✿ **a watering can or jug**

✿ **a see-through polythene bag**

✿ **an elastic band or string**

1. Cut off the top of the pineapple, so that you get the leaves and about 1cm of the flesh. Leave the top to dry for a couple of days. While this is happening you can pig out on the rest of the pineapple!

Mmm!

2. Cover your work area with newspaper. Mix your compost with a handful of sand and fill your pot with the stuff.

3. Pop your pineapple top in the pot and bury the flesh. Water and cover the whole thing with a polythene bag. Tie the bag on with an elastic band or string.

4. Put in a warm spot and if you're lucky new leaves should soon begin to appear at the centre. When this happens, remove the bag. Pineapple plants just hate the cold, so make sure that you keep it warm throughout its life. If you are very lucky after a year or two it might even reward you with a flower.

Go nutty

Next time you snack on fresh peanuts (the sort that come in their shells and are for some reason called monkey nuts) save a few for planting. Before too long you could be feasting on your very own home-grown nuts! April is the best time to start sowing.

You will need

- ✿ **a handful of peanuts in shells**
- ✿ **newspaper**
- ✿ **potting compost**
- ✿ **a large pot**
- ✿ **a watering can or jug**
- ✿ **a see-through polythene bag**
- ✿ **an elastic band or string**

1. Carefully crack all your peanut shells (be careful not to crush the poor little nuts). Cracking the shells will allow water to get at the nuts.

crack!

2. Cover your work area with newspaper. Fill a large pot with compost and use your finger to poke a series of holes (about 1.5cm deep) towards the centre of the pot. Push the nuts into the holes and cover with compost.

3. Water and cover with a polythene bag. Secure the bag with an elastic band or string.

4. Put in a warm place (near a radiator is ideal) and within two or three weeks the peanuts should begin to sprout.

5. Remove the polythene bag and move to a sunny windowsill. Water regularly and if you're lucky it should produce yellow flowers in the summer. Once these die back, seed pods should appear. This is when it gets interesting because it will actually plant its own nuts by pushing these pods into the soil. The nuts will eventually ripen under the soil. Soon you could be absolutely surrounded by nuts!

Crafty Ideas

Now's the time to reach for the scrap box, get out your glue stick and get ready to make some **Flower Power** works of art!

Flower Power pot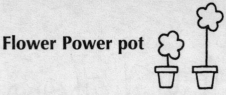

Sunflowers really are a great design to put on things, so why not brighten up a few boring old flowerpots with them?

<u>You will need</u>

- ✿ **newspaper**
- ✿ **a small clay or plastic flowerpot**
- ✿ **white primer paint**
- ✿ **a paintbrush**
- ✿ **a pencil**
- ✿ **card, for stencil**
- ✿ **a craft knife**
- ✿ **sticky tape**
- ✿ **yellow and orange ceramic paint**
- ✿ **a sponge**

1. Cover your work surfaces with newspaper. If you're using a clay flowerpot, paint the whole thing with white primer paint to stop the clay soaking up the other colours. Leave to dry.

2. Make a tiny sunflower stencil, by tracing the template. Transfer it to the card and get your grown-up to cut out the stencil with a craft knife.

3. Tape the stencil to the side of the pot and dab on paint with the sponge – orange for the centre and yellow for the petals. Leave the stencil on until the paint is dry, then stencil some more sunflowers around the pot.

4. Finally paint the rim orange and before you know it you will be the proud owner of a positively picturesque pot.

These pots also make great pressies – mums just love them!

How lovely!

Pressing business

Pressing flowers and leaves is a fab way of keeping them to brighten up miserable winter days. However, some things are more suitable for pressing than others. Don't expect to be able to press a sunflower head – but you could press some petals! On the other hand, pressing is the ideal way of preserving your nasturtiums!

Hmm!

You will need

✿ cardboard

✿ scissors

✿ corrugated cardboard

✿ newspaper

✿ flowers or leaves

✿ string

1. Cut out two bits of cardboard, two bits of corrugated cardboard and loads of sheets of newspaper all the same size.

2. Start building up your press. Lay a bit of corrugated card on a bit of cardboard, then top this with newspaper. Lay your flowers or leaves on top of the newspaper, then cover with more newspaper. Place the other bit of corrugated card on top of the newspaper and finally top the whole lot with the last bit of card.

3. Tie two bits of string tightly around the press, then place under a whole stack of books. Leave for at least two weeks, then take out the flowers and make into a cool card or stunning picture.

All dried up

If you loved your sunflowers so much that you couldn't bear to let them go, why not try drying a few!

You will need

✿ **a sunflower**

✿ **a wood saw**

✿ **string**

1. When your sunflower heads are quite small and before any seeds begin to form, get an adult to hack one down. Make sure that they leave about 40cm of stalk.

2. Tie some string around the stem and hang from the ceiling in a dark, warm place – a loft with a slightly open window is ideal. Leave them for about a month to dry out completely.

3. Once your sunflower is fully dry you can display it in a suitable pot and bring a little sunshine into your life!

Flowery paper

Make some totally original paper with bits of old newspaper and ironed nasturtium flowers. Yes ironed!

You will need

✿ **lovely fresh nasturtium flowers**

✿ **2 sheets of kitchen paper**

✿ **an iron**

✿ **old newspaper**

✿ **a bucket**

✿ **water**

✿ **a sieve**

✿ **a liquidizer (optional)**

✿ **tea towels**

✿ **a rolling pin**

✿ **a plastic bag**

✿ **loads of heavy books**

1. Lay the fresh flowers between the two sheets of kitchen paper and point your grown-up in the direction of the iron. Iron until the flowers are completely dry.

2. Cut newspaper into small bits and put into the bucket with lots of water. Leave to soak for 24 hours.

3. Drain through a sieve, then mix to a pulp (gooey mess) with your hands. Soak the pulp in water once more – just for a couple of hours this time – then drain again. If you want to get finer looking paper, you could ask a grown-up to whizz the goo through a liquidizer at this stage!

squelch!

4. Now add the ironed nasturtiums and mix around a little. Don't worry if they break up.

5. Put the pulp on a tea towel and roll out with a rolling pin.

6. Cover the flattened pulp with another tea towel and then a plastic bag. Then squash the whole lot down with a mountain of heavy books. Leave to dry for at least a day and before you know it you will have some real FLOWER POWER paper! This paper looks great made into cards or wrapping paper.

Seedy box

Make this funky sunflower box, then pop a few seeds inside and give someone a little of their very own Flower Power!

<u>You will need</u>

- ✿ **a round box, such as the ones cheese triangles come in**
- ✿ **coloured paper**
- ✿ **a glue stick**
- ✿ **yellow and brown crêpe paper (or other paper)**
- ✿ **a few small seeds**
- ✿ **a few large sunflower seeds suitable for growing**

1. Using your box as a template, cut out enough coloured paper to cover the outside of your box. Glue the paper in position, remembering not to stick the two halves together!

2. Cut out a brown circle of crêpe paper to make the centre of the flower. Stick it over the top of the box.

3. Cut out loads of petal shapes from the yellow crêpe paper and stick them around the circle. Two or three layers of petals make it look great!

4. Put a few dabs of glue on the brown centre and stick some seeds there. Pop a few of your harvested seeds in the box and give this pressie to a friend!